D0843325

Buildings on the Farm

by Teddy Borth

ABDO
ON THE FARM
Kids

Visit us at www.abdopublishing.com

Published by Abdo Kids, a division of ABDO, PO Box 398166, Minneapolis, Minnesota 55439.

Copyright © 2015 by Abdo Consulting Group, Inc. International copyrights reserved in all countries.
No part of this book may be reproduced in any form without written permission from the publisher.

Printed in the United States of America, North Mankato, Minnesota.

032014

092014

PRINTED ON RECYCLED PAPER

Photo Credits: Shutterstock, Thinkstock

Production Contributors: Teddy Borth, Jennie Forsberg, Grace Hansen

Design Contributors: Dorothy Toth, Laura Rask

Library of Congress Control Number: 2013952560

Cataloging-in-Publication Data

Borth, Teddy.

 Buildings on the farm / Teddy Borth.

   p. cm. -- (On the farm)

ISBN 978-1-62970-051-9 (lib. bdg.)

Includes bibliographical references and index.

1. Farm buildings--Juvenile literature.   I. Title.

631.2--dc23

                    2013952560

Table of Contents

Buildings on the Farm

There are many buildings on the farm. Animals, people, and tools all need homes!

The Barn

The barn is big and open.

A barn can hold many

things. A barn is a place

for the farmer to work.

Animals can live in the barn. Tractors can be found in the barn. A barn can store **crops**.

8

9

The Chicken Coop

Chickens live in the chicken coop. The chicken coop looks like a small house.

11

Hens lay eggs in the chicken coop. The coop also protects chickens from bad weather.

The Silo

Silos are very tall.

Silos are round.

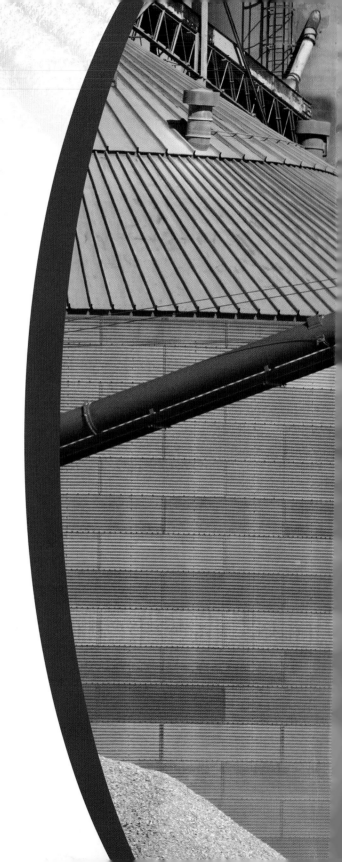

Farmers keep what they grow in the **silo**. The silo keeps the **harvest** safe.

16

17

The Stable

Horses live in the **stable**.

Stables can be open or

have a roof.

Each horse has a spot in the **stable**. These spots are called **stalls**.

More Facts

- Barns are typically the oldest building on the farm.

- **Stables** are historically the second oldest building type on the farm.

- The tallest **silo** is in Germany and is about 394 feet (120 m) tall.

- "Free range" animals can roam freely outdoors for at least part of the day.

Glossary

crops – any plant that is grown and gathered.

harvest – ripe crop that is gathered.

silo – a round building that farmers use for storing corn and grain.

stable – a building where horses live and eat.

stall – a small area in the stable that fits one animal.

23

Index

abdokids.com

Use this code to log on to abdokids.com and access crafts, games, videos and more!

Abdo Kids Code:
OBK0519